Minecraft

The Ultimate Players Guide To Minecraft

By Ultimate App Guidebooks

Introduction

Minecraft is a simple sandbox style game where the player is free to roam wherever they choose creating worlds with blocks. The game can be played in various different modes like Survival, Creative, Adventure and Hardcore. Minecraft has grown so much now, that it's possible to change the game completely with third party mods (modifications) that can change the textures, appearance and gameplay of the game. Minecraft was originally created by Markus "Notch" Persson a Swedish programmer, before being taken on by Majong who later developed and published it to the general public. It was released on the PC in 2009 in its alpha stage before being updated for its full release in 2011.

In that year Minecraft deservedly received 5 awards in the 2011 Game Developers Conference, it was awarded the Best Downloadable Game, Best Debut game Award, Audience Award, Grand Prize and Innovation Award. By the end of 2013 the game had sold over 12 million copies for the PC and 33 million copies on all the other devices.

The Minecraft world is broken up into different regions ranging from snowfields, to hot deserts and jungles. The game features a daytime/night-time cycle which lasts 20 minutes for one full cycle. During the daytime, players encounter non hostile characters such as animals like cows, pigs and chickens which can be used for food and for crafting materials. But as night time comes in, the scene changes leading to more hostile characters to emerge in the shape of large spiders, zombies, skeletons and other creatures. This survival mode to the game is what forces a player to use the material's around them, to create homes, forts and other protection to survive in the game.

When entering the game, a brand new world is randomly created for the player. This set point is a spawn spot that the player will return to, until the player builds him or herself a home and rests in bed. From that time on this becomes the players new fixed spawn point. As the player moves around exploring the world, more land to explore is generated around them. The world is created in chunks which are 16x16 squares of blocks. The most common material of these blocks are stone, sand and dirt. The aim of this game is to craft these blocks into items that can be used by the player.

This open ended game play is one of the most appealing things to the Minecraft game, where the game is only limited by the imagination of the player. Now with the addition of third party modifications, the doors of the Minecraft world have been blown wide open. For example type the search term "Minecraft" into Youtube.com and you'll find a huge treasure trove of videos from player's all over the world displaying their Minecraft creations to the world.

But enough about that, you already know this, you're a fan of Minecraft and you want more from the game. Firstly, while this book is titled as the "Ultimate Guide To Minecraft" it could never cover every little thing about Minecraft. With the speed with which the internet, technology and the Minecraft game is evolving, this book couldn't possibly give you everything you need to know. And honestly would you really want to be reading this book instead of playing the game...we thought so!

So what can you discover from this book?

Inside we'll show you how to get more from Minecraft, tips on building homes, tips on fighting enemies, tips on surviving at night time and the nether region, how to install Minecraft mods on your PC, and finally a world of Minecraft resources that every Minecraft player should really know about.

Think that could really help you out? We thought so, now let's get stuck in...

HOUSE BUILDING IN MINECRAFT: TIPS

Few items are more important or interesting in your Minecraft reality that your home. Not only can you design wonderful living areas, but these can be enhanced and beautified to reflect your desires and really put a personal touch on your game playing experience.

However, looks aside, the house provides one essential service in the Minecraft universe and that is one of a safe haven. A place where you can craft, store treasure, get a good night sleep and above all else protect yourself from all the nasty monsters that roam freely at night. The only way to survive in Minecraft is to have shelter. Regardless of the turrets, spires or elaborate design you may eventually build, the essential aspect to remember is protection. That is the true purpose of the build.

Beginners - As you spawn in the Minecraft universe everything looks wonderful. The block sun is shining above and blocky animals are frolicking in the fields. Your virtual world seems calm, danger free, simply a great place. Unfortunately, night arrives at break neck speed and your basic need must be taken care of, namely shelter. If you do not procure this essential component of Minecraft life you will not make it through the night; guaranteed! So let's look at a few tips that will help you get through that first day and night.

Shelter Is The Name Of The Game - Your first day was likely spent gathering material but you don't have enough time or crafted material to build a house. No worries! A hole in the ground of a dug out side of a mountain will get you through your first night. When entering the hole make certain that you have blocked all entrance points; Zombies have a way of finding a way into your area.

Choose Your Material Wisely - As with most things that which comes easiest is rarely the best. The most readily found materials, (i.e. dirt, sand and wood), do not make for very safe houses. Dirt and sand are to be avoided at all costs as they are easily destroyed by TNT and can actually collapse due to gravity. You can make your house out of wood planks as trees are abundant, but although these structures are aesthetically appeasing they provide little defense against fire or explosion. If you want to build something to last get some cobble-stone. To do so, create a wooden pickaxe, and mine soft stone, which is gray in appearance. This is the strongest material that is easily mined. The look might not be the best but it usefulness outweighs this fact.

Keep It Simple - Your fist house should have the basics: Four walls, a roof and a door. A place to craft and sleep is what we want. A bed is very important as it can turn night into day and allow for a quick return to the daytime mining.

Advanced - Once you have created a basic home and are safe from the nasty creatures you share your world with, you can now look to improve your surroundings and put a personal touch to your house. There are still certain aspects to remember while making these changes.

Added Protection- As the game progresses you will notice that creatures such as creepers can have a nasty habit of blowing up the walls of your house. You can reduce this risk by added blast resistant materials to the outside of your house. One of the least time consuming ways of doing this is by encasing your structure in water. Water has a very high explosive resistance. Creating waterfalls and moats are a great way to protect your home. Obsidian is also good bet and bedrock is the ultimate, although it requires quite a lot of digging to get at.

Must Have Rooms - Besides a bedroom there should be a few selected rooms that will make game play that much better.

Crafting Room - This should include chests with materials need to craft items that are regularly required. This room should also include a furnace with separate chests for materials that must be smelted as well as for fuel, be it lava or coal.

Treasure Room - The name is a bit of a misnomer as this room does not only contain treasures. I suggest you conceal this room and keep all your most valuable weapons, armor, tools and materials. You never know when all hell might break loose, it is better to have a safe place for all your goodies.

Storage Room - This is an ideal place to put all of the easily obtained materials. It is wise to have even the base materials easily accessible in a safe environment.

Defences And Style - Once all the elements are present you can let your imagination run wild. Walls of pure diamonds, turrets and towers reaching skyward, lava flows heating water for spas, water slides and perhaps a roller coaster to add some excitement. The fact is the possibilities are endless. Once you create this castle you might want to go the extra mile and protect it with sentinels. Golems make wonderful guardians. You must sequester them and allow space for them to attack, but they have quite a few hit points and attack with a lot of power. You can also work in a myriad of traps; arrow slits and murder holes to add to your protection and authenticity of your keep.

Once you have mastered your building techniques and have created a safe place to craft, store and sleep, you can look to expand and build a farm connected to your house. This will assure a readily available food supply and provide a controlled area for seeds. You can be-come more ambitious and build an entire village, or perhaps just a secondary house next to a pond, or by the seaside. The beauty of the game is that your imagination is the only limitation, so expand your horizons, gather and go wild with you creations. You can truly mold the landscape to your desire.

MINECRAFT AT NIGHT

Minecraft is a wonderful game that allows you to completely immerse yourself in a world of your own creation. Everything you need to construct a wonderful universe is at your disposal. All you need to do is mine material, transform, or craft them, into object to suit your needs and let your imagination run wild. This is accomplished without any problem during the day time hours.

The sun will eventually go down however, and when this occurs the peaceful environment transforms into a dangerous place filled with monsters roaming across the countryside. These creatures have one main agenda; to hurt you. All of these brutes spawn at night and they are near impossible to avoid. The logical question that must be asked is: what can you do at night to avoid being injured and make it to the rising of a new day?

Feet Were Made For Running - Although not the recommended defense against all the antagonists lurking in the dark, you can avoid contact with the beasts by legging it! The problem this poses is the fact that making out the surrounding terrain might be an issue. In the dark, it is rather difficult to see potential escape routes. If you choose to mine at night and are planning on dashing to safety if attacked, it would be prudent to place some torches in the adjacent area in order to shed light on your possible escape routes. Using this technique adds an interesting element to the game; it provides an adrenaline rush! Even though you are in a virtual, blocky world, running for your life always gets the blood flowing.

Attack! - This is an exciting way to take care of your visitor problem. It does involve a few key components, namely weapons that will allow you to inflict damage on your foes. At the beginning of your game it is easy to craft a simple wooden sword. Although not the strongest of materials, this will cause enough damage to vanquish your foes in a couple of hits. Once more there is a sense of satisfaction in dealing with your enemies in this way.

Of course there are creatures like skeletons who attack with range weapons. They can inflict damage with an arrow from quite a distance. If you only have melee weapons it could prove difficult to get rid of these foes. I suggest a combination of these first two techniques in or-der to assure that every type of potential enemy can be taken care of. So be ready to attack, but have your running shoes on in case the need arise.

Water Is Your Friend - An important tid-bit of information to keep in mind is that these evil creatures cannot spawn in water. What this means is that if you can spend the night on the water you will be safe. The only MOB that can be born in water is the squid. Although these look rather menacing, they will not attack you. They can provide you with ink if you need but pose no danger. If you choose to take this option to get through the night, simply swim out to the middle of a body of water and got down to the bottom.

Once there create a tower of blocks right up to the surface of the water. You can then add blocks to the tower to create a platform. This will provide you a nice place to examine what is happening on dry land from the safety of the water.

Arrows may still reach you if you are not far enough from the shore, but a simple wall placed between you and the shoreline will make this point moot. This water platform can be used as a dock for a boat as you advance in the game.

Dig A Hole/ Build A house - The surest way to avoid all of the nasty night time visitors is to create a shelter for yourself. This can be a simple hole dug into the ground, a hollowed out side of a hill, a simple box like above ground dwelling or an elaborate house that can rival any castle you may have dreamed of as a child. The important thing to remember is that if you are in the safety of your dwelling the creatures cannot get at you and inflict damage.

Once in these safe places you can continue to mine within the walls without worries. Although there is a chance that you may stumble upon an underground cave if you dig too deep, that could be teeming with spiders or other monsters, there is no real danger. This is the safest way to spend the night although it is not nearly as exciting as the other solutions.

Eventually you will have built a house and will spend most nights within its confines. More-over once you craft a bed you can immediately change night into day simply by going to sleep. This is a viable way to maintain the safest environment possible but it also makes the game rather dull. If the world is stripped of some of its most evil denizens you are removing that which makes the game exciting. In my opinions build a house you can even craft a bed, just do not use it. Embrace the night!

Once you have taken a small piece of your world and created a homestead you should spend the night mining the surrounding area. If you are visited by a zombie hoard or an army of skeletons, you will have the safety of your home nearby. Furthermore, if you planned your house intelligently, you may have put in some arrow slits or other creative ways to eradicate your enemies while not placing yourself at risk. Do not hide behind your stone, wooden or even diamond walls, roam free at night, the world you have created belongs to you and not them!

EFFECTIVELY FIGHTING ENEMIES IN MINECRAFT

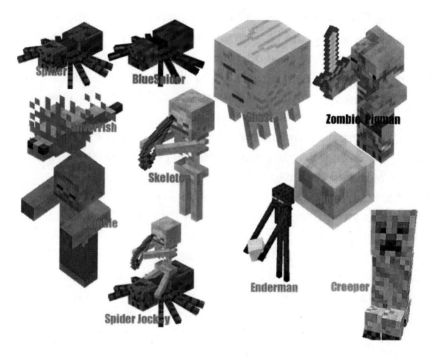

Once you have crafted your home and mined to your heart's content, you are likely spending evenings in your bed avoiding the night time nastiness of the spawned MOBS, well if you are feeling that the game has become a little redundant, or you are looking for a thrill, get out of your bed sheets and go and fight the creatures that have kept you huddled in your home. Before you do so however, you must prepare yourself for the battles to come.

Preparation - The most important thing to have at your disposal is a weapon. Craft a sword, out of stone if possible, get a bow, don some armor and even bring along a few tamed wolves if you have them.

You may also want to grab a few torches before you head out. On the more practical side you can set the difficulty to easy in the options screen. This can be changed to a more challenging setting once you have perfected your fighting technique.

Learning How To Strike: - There are several ways of approaching the fights with your Minecraft enemies. If you so choose, and you have the required equipment, you can try and destroy them from a distance with your bow. If this is not an option and you must use your sword, it would be wise to learn how to perform a critical strike. A critical strike is performed by jumping or falling toward your opponent and hitting him while you are still in the air. This may demand a bit of practice in order to get the timing down.
Now that the basics are covered let's look at a few tricks you may use to vanquish specific types of monsters.

Zombies - Zombies are the easiest creatures to destroy. Their movements are slow and they will ignite in the daytime sun. The technique is simple, once the zombie is within two blocks of you, jump and perform a critical strike. There is no need to retreat after striking as the zombie is too slow to counterstrike. Repeat this sequence until your foe is dead.

Skeletons - Skeletons have the added danger of carrying bows and can attack you from a distance. The good thing is that when they are far enough the arrows are avoidable. If you have a bow you can send a few volleys his way and eradicate the problem that way. If not, approach your enemy and be prepared to block the arrow with a right click of the mouse. Once you are close enough time the speed at which he is firing and deliver critical strikes when he is reloading. It is important to remember that Skeletons also burn in daylight.

Spiders - Spiders are a little trickier that the previous two creatures because they can climb and do not burn with the morning sun. In fact you can encounter them during the day, but as long as you keep a safe distance they will remain passive during the day. The important technique to utilize with spiders is to run at it. If the beast begins to climb give it a running hit to bring it back down. When on the ground, keep moving towards it, swinging the sword as you go. You may take some damage this way, but you will also deliver running strikes and quickly be done with your arachnid foe.

Creepers - Creepers are dangerous. They move silently and will explode if they are near you. These are made to be killed with a bow. If the bow is not part of your equipment. You must use your sword. When swinging at a Creeper make sure that you back away after you hit it. If he begins to flash and get bigger, run away quickly as he is getting ready to blow. It should me mentioned that there also charged Creepers, They have a bluish aura around them. These creatures carry twice the explosive potential of regular Creepers so be warned.

Endermen - These tall black enemies can teleport and can cause quite a bit of damage with their hits. Their weakness is water. They sustain damage by water and usually die in the rain. When facing an Endermen try to avoid eye contact, which means do not place your crosshairs over its upper body. If you manage this run towards it and deliver a critical strike. This will likely cause your enemy to teleport. You can locate the Endermen by following the trail of particles left behind. Once located repeat the procedure. Conversely you can step in the water and make eye contact. This will cause your enemy to teleport to you and sustain damage by the water. You can continue to do this until he is vanquished.

Spider Jockey - These creatures are basically a skeleton riding a spider. I suggest you take care of the skeleton first, preferably with a bow. You can then deal with the spider following the regular procedure.

Silverfish - These pesky little creatures are found in strongholds. To make matters worse they hide in blocks. If you happen to break a block they are in, they will attack you and so will any of their family in the vicinity. If you are in a stronghold and you notice a block is breaking too easily there is a silverfish in it. Stop and back away. If you have TNT you can blow up these weakened, silverfish laden blocks and eliminate the threat altogether. If you are entangled with a swarm of these things, the best bet is to run away and return at a later time.

Slime - Slime is an easily vanquished foe that loves far underground. A small slime will die with one sword swipe. It is a good idea to take them down with your bare hands as this will prolong your sword's life. If you encounter a large slime, it will separate into two medium slimes after it is hit, which will separate into two small slimes each. Remember small slimes cause no damage, so try and get the larger ones down to the manageable size.

This covers the most common monsters in Minecraft, you may see different enemies when you delved in to the nether region, but the technique remains the same.

MINECRAFT HELL – THE NETHER

The Nether, a dimension in Minecraft where flames shoot up from the ground, lakes of lava form the floor and a whole slew of new monsters await. There is no natural light in the Nether. The eerie glow of the lava and glowstones bathe the landscape in a strange orange hue. This is not your regular Minecraft world, it is its evil counterpart: it is its version of hell. This should not deter your investigation of this fascinating area, on the contrary it should excite the player to enjoy yet another intricate element of the game.

Getting to the Nether - In order to get to the Nether you must first construct a portal. These are created by building a frame out of Obsidian blocks. You must lay out 4 blocks on the ground. Then place four blocks going upward ON the Obsidian located at the extremities of your 4 block line. Once done simply join the top pieces of your construction and you will have a frame with a 2x3 opening in the center. Take out your flint and steel and set the opening on fire. This will create your portal and give you access to the Nether. Any type of explosion will break your portal as will water or lava poured into its opening.

Moving around in the Nether - The Nether mimics the regular Overworld area in the game with one crucial difference. The distances are scaled down. Moving one block in the Nether is equivalent to 8 blocks in the Overworld. This allows for potential short cuts to different areas. Of course traveling through the Nether is no walk in the park, and sometimes the longer, sun filled walk in the normal environment in a more pleasant solution. The terrain in the Nether is much less uniform than in the regular world. A series of platforms usually make up the ground and these are separated by fire blasts and lava pool, not the easiest place for a stroll. Venture at your own risk!

Monsters in the Nether - As you would expect the Nether has its own set of nasty creatures. These have the common power of being completely fire-proof and can often be seen wandering out of lava. Here is a list of the creatures you can expect to encounter in your travels through the underworld.

Ghasts - These are huge monsters that resemble flying jellyfish. If any of these 4x4x4 giants see a player they will shoot fireballs at it. Luckily these can be deflected back at the Ghast with a well-placed arrow, punching or hitting them with any tool. When a Ghast is struck by his rebounded fireball he will explode and leave a crater. You can also get rid of them with a couple of arrows. They can provide gun powder and ghast tears.

Zombie Pigmen - These creatures tend to come to be in groups and wander aimlessly around the Nether. They will not attack unless provoked. If this occurs all Zombie Pigmen in a 32 block area will sprint at the player if he is within 16 blocks. This can cause some issues as they are in a group and might come at you from your blind side. When vanquished you can get some rotten flesh, a gold nugget or even a gold ingot. They will sometimes drop some other golden items like swords or helmets which may even be enchanted!

Blazes - These are found in Nether Fortresses. The can shoot 3 fireballs in rapid fashion and also have the ability to float. When they are readying for a volley they will appear to catch fire. This can provide the player with a warning prior to being attacked. They will provide you with Blaze rods.

Magma Cubes - These are the warm blooded spring-like cousins of the Overworld Slimes. Much like their green family members they will break down into smaller versions of the original if they are struck. These, relatively, rare creatures will provide magma cream if dropped.

Wither Skeletons - These are the Nether version of Skeletons. They have two distinct features. Firstly, they are bigger, standing over two blocks tall and carry stone swords rather than bows. They also have the power to infect a player when they hit them. This acts like a poison that darkens the health bars and causes additional damage for a few seconds. When they are defeated they may leave some coal and bones behind.

Blocks found in the Nether - As you would suspect there are also blocks that are specific to the Nether.

Netherrack - An infinitely burning block, it is the main block found in the Nether. These can be set on fire and replace torches.

Soul Sand - This is a brown block that slows the movement of however is walking over it. It can be used to make docks, one way doors and mine-cart only passages.

Glowstones - These golden blocks glow. When mined they produce Glowstone Dust which is used in making potions and redstone lamps.

Nether Brick - A dark purple block that resembles a brick. These can be used to fashion a Nether Fence.

Other Oddities
- Certain materials are affected by the Nether. For example, there is no way to place water in the Nether. If you use a bucket you will end up with steam and an empty bucket.
- Trees can grow but their leaves will be brown and dead-looking.

- Compasses and clock can be brought into the Nether. The problem is that, since they are now in a different dimension, they will not work.
- Beds are unusable as they will blow up if a player attempts to sleep in them.
- You can encounter some Overworld MOBS in the Nether. These were not spawned but either wandered through the portal or were pushed through.
- Throwing eggs and constructing golem's works normally in the Nether. Snow Golems are impossible to create as they will melt in the hellish surroundings.
- There is no day/night cycle and there is no weather in the Nether.

Now you have the information needed to venture into Minecraft hades, Good luck!

MINECRAFT FOR TABLETS

Minecraft for portable devices, or Minecraft PE (pocket edition) is a popular scaled down version of the PC or Xbox 360 game. While the goal of the game remains the same there are several omissions that make the game a little different. There are many aspect that had to be adjusted because of the use of a touchscreen control system.

The world is finite, it lacks many of the biomes and structures that are found in the PC version. The Nether does not exist in the Pocket Edtion, but there is a Nether Reactor. The crafting itself is altered using the Minecraft Advanced Touch Technology Interface System (MATTIS) for this purpose. Rather than the regular 2x2 and 3x3 grids, four categories appear down the left side: Blocks, Tools, Food and Armor, and Decoration.

By touching these categories you get a list of craft-able items or blocks.
Each of these is followed by a list of required materials for that particular crafting. Beside these main features that are different there are more subtle differences as well.

Differences To Look For
- Roses are of a cyan colour in the PE version. These are called roses but cannot be crafted into dye.
- The average range for placing or destroying a block is increased. On the PC version this was limited to 4-6 on the PE version it is 6-9.
- Skeletons seem sluggish. They are less accurate or fast than in the other versions of the game.
- Zombie Pigmen are not neutral. They will attack a player on sight and can administer quite a large amount of damage.

These are little differences and do not really take anything away from the game. It is enjoyable to notice them and keep them in mind as they may affect your game play and decisions.

Game Play Tips
- This game saps a lot of power. It is wise to make sure that your battery is fully charged when commencing a session or, better yet, plugged into the wall.
- Before you seek out any battles of link up with someone else, it would be a good idea to get used to the control system. Moving around with a touchscreen control system is tricky to the uninitiated can be very tricky. You would not want to face any danger until this aspect is truly mastered.
- If you do run into a bunch of hostile monsters, or if you are having issues with any nasty creature, you can turn the Peaceful mode on.
- Diamonds are very deep, right near the bedrock. Don't lose hope, just keep digging! Once you are down to the 10th to 16th layer you should find some.

- Invite friends over and link up into a game with them. This is a fun way to enjoy the game with someone else or. Even better, hold some epic battles with one another.

The creators of the Minecraft world are constantly trying to bring the pocket edition up to par with the other versions. There are regular updates that make the game resemble the PC version. There are limitations when dealing with a handheld device but the game play is already more than acceptable and if these developments continue it can only get better!

Minecraft XBOX 360

Xbox 360 is currently the only console that carries Minecraft. There will be a version for the new Xbox One and there has been rumors about the game appearing on the Sony family of consoles but for now it is only on Xbox 360. The game is well worth trying as the controls are easy and the game play is essentially equal to the PC version. There are a few differences between the two versions, but these do not really deter from the experience.

Differences When Compared To PC

- The crafting style differs from that of the PC version. There are similarities between the PC's crafting grids, but the interface does not need a gamer to put the items in a specific place or order. The game simply informs the user what is required to craft a selected item. If the player has the required blocks, the game will craft the desired object.
- The difficulty level of a world cannot be changed while in the game. You may alter the setting when choosing the

world you wish to play in at the beginning of a gaming session.
- The console version includes a tutorial mode. This is useful to most newcomers to the game. The tutorial covers most of the basics and even brings the players to build their first house and thus survive the night.
- A map is provided when you begin a new world.
- There is the capacity of playing in a split screen mode. (Up to 4 players can play in this mode.)
- The world itself is limited in size. This might change with subsequent updates, but for now it is limited to a 864X864 grid. As you would suspect the Nether is also limited. Distances in the Nether versus the surface world are 1:3 in this version. This makes the Nether about 288X288 in size. The End is similar in size.
- Players enjoying the Creative Mode setting can sprint while flying in this version.
- Breeding and spawning works like in the PC version, except the number of tamed Wolves and Snow Golems is limited to 8. Snow Golems will attack Creepers, so be wary of their placement.

Tips and Tricks:

- Unlimited water supply can be created by making a 2X2 square 1 block deep then placing water on two opposite corners.
- Land animals will spawn on your property if it has grass.
- If you are digging and hear multiple MOBS, there is likely a hidden cave near where you are digging. Be wary!
- These MOBS can also spawn in your house if it is not well lit. Keep those torches burning.
- Boats will always go up to the top of a body of water. If you are near a waterfall this can make a handy elevator.

- You can preserve you pickaxe by switching between picks when mining. Only the pick being used when a block collapses is given damage.
- Do not hesitate to build canals of flowing water. This can be done by using signs or other blocks to contain the water. Then you can ride the waves in a boat and travel and a quickened pace through your world.
- Try to craft your doors from the outside of your house. This prevents the MOBS from getting into your doorstep.
- If you build a wooden structure out of stacked wooden slabs it becomes a fireproof wooden creation.
- Fire can kill MOBS without them ever attacking you.

These tips are just the beginning there are a myriad of other tricks that can work in the Xbox version of the game. Do not be fearful of trying new things. The beauty of this game is that everything is possible and you imagination is the only limiting factor on what you can create. Go crazy and build an entire world that fits your desires. The only danger is the game may become too addictive and you will never be able to turn the console off.

MINECRAFT TIPS AND TRICKS

Minecraft began rather modestly. It was a simple game based where you could mine materials and craft a world of your own desire. What may not have been expected when the game first appeared was its world wide appeal. The game has gone through numerous up-grades and has truly become a universe of its own with fascinating creatures and locales. As with any video game however there are certain tips, hints or tricks that can make the play much more interesting. Here are a few tips that will help you get a better experience form your gameplay.

Tips for Building
Try and build near a landmark. You must remember that the world in large and it is easy to lose yourself. Alternately you can build your place in such a way that it is visible from quite a distance. House equals safety so it is a good idea to always be aware of its location.

Do not hesitate to build your mine within the walls of your house. This will provide protection and you will have easy access to your preferred digging site.

Creepers can blow up entire walls of your abode. Build a moat or protective wall around your house to prevent this unfortunate event. A lava moat is an interesting alternative, it provides protection and is damaging to most creatures you will meet.

Build on a mountain to provide a clear view of your surroundings.

Once you are proficient with your building skills, challenge yourself to build something from the real world. The Sears Tower for example. It makes for a much richer experience.

Traveling Tips
One of the funniest parts of the game is exploring the vast environment. This will take you far from the safety of your home or castle. There are a few things that will make your treks out into the wilderness a positive adventure.

It would be a good idea to bring extra tools. Tools and weapons have a limited lifespan in the game. When traveling the countryside, mining and fighting along the way, there is a high probability that your tools and weapons will wear out. There is nothing more frustrating than needing a certain tool and not having the materials to craft it. A few spares, crafted at home, where most of your materials are hoarded, is the best way to avoid this problem. It could also be a good idea to bring a chest to store some of the items you will find on your voyage.

Be aware of your surroundings while you are on the move. There are caves and secret underground cave systems that provide rare materials. Make your travels worth-while and try not to miss these opportunities when they come your way. Do not spent an inordinate amount of time on building a shelter. A simple hole in the ground, or hollowed out square in a hillside will suffice. If you waste your time making elaborate shelters in all corners of the world, you will have very little time for exploration.

Survival Tips
The game is filled with dangerous monsters that will cause a great deal of harm. There are however, other types of dangers that can cause quite a lot of damage but can be avoided. Digging straight downward should be avoided. The Minecraft world is littered with underground chambers. These can be populated by a bunch of monsters or be filled with a large lava lake. Either way, accidentally falling into these areas is not a desired outcome of mining. Mine a few blocks ahead of yourself so you can be aware of any of these un-wanted secret chambers are present.

Do not dig straight up. Or at least, do not dig if you are not using an iron or diamond shovel. Gravel and sand will suffocate anyone who mines them from below in rapid fashion. A quick and powerful shovel is the only way to survive.
Be on the look out for creepers! These soundless devils can get the drop on you when you least expect it and their exploding personality will do quite a lot of damage if the opportunity presents itself.

Save your food for when you really need it. Do not devour your food stuff arbitrarily, wait until you're down at least 4 food indicators.

Do not be hesitate to eat a spider's eye if you are in a bad way. This will poison you for 5 seconds but will regenerate your health. Rotten flesh has the same sort of result. It is not as effective as food, but does have some positive, recuperative elements. These are not to be taken instead of real food if you have some at hand, but they will help you to survive in a pinch.

Make sure you have mastered the art of jumping before you attempt any large leaps. This may seems obvious, but, in my experience, most people try to jump dangerous obstacles when they are ill prepared. This leads only to a lot of pain! Be wary of strangers: There could be some people you meet who are not there to help you and will, if given the chance, they may even attack you in order to take over your materials or even your home. Keep up your vigilance and only trust those you know.

If you venture into a cave, be sure to mark your way out. It is easy to get turned around in the caves and you may spent quite a long time trying to get out.

Once you are an advanced player, it would be a good idea to create a safe area in order to grow your own food and plants. When done in a controlled area, safe from the pitfalls of the game, you will never lack food or plant material.
These are just a few tricks and tips that you should consider when venturing into this game. There are so many different layers to this game that it is impossible to list all of the potential tricks to making your gameplay more enjoyable. Experience will provide you with some of your own techniques and you will discover your own ways of maintain your interest in the game.

MINECRAFT MODS

Minecraft mods (or modifications) are additional ways to get much more from the game. There are various different ways in which people use mods, some to change the way the game looks and others to how it behaves. Some modifications can include simple things such as shading or texture packs to more advanced options like expansions that bring in experiences and features from other games or worlds. With the popularity of Minecraft there are now hundreds if not thousands of modifications that are out there to try out.

But a word of warning first though, while mods are a great way to get much from the game, some do come with a risk. Most Minecraft modifications are produced by outside sources not linked to the game, usually Minecraft fans themselves.
This can cause problems as some (although a very small number) can contain badly written code or viruses that can damage or bring your whole Minecraft world crashing down.

But with that word or warning out of the way, a visit to some of the more reliable and popular Minecraft site and forum hangouts, should keep you far from trouble.

Popular Modifications
Here's some links to some popular texture pack modification you might want to try out...

Legend Of Zelda Texture Pack – Zelda themed Minecraft modification. http://bit.ly/1f5HqgL

Halo Wars – Halo themed Minecraft texture pack. http://bit.ly/1f5Hv49

Star Wars Inspired Texture Pack – If you love all things Star Wars this modification is one you're sure to enjoy. http://bit.ly/1iJoQjs

MarioCraft - If you're a fan of New Super Mario Bros, this is a great mod to change the Minecraft world to look like the famous game. http://bit.ly/1eX2lC5

If that isn't enough for you, here's a packed with tons of popular Minecraft mods that will totally transform your Minecraft game forever... http://bit.ly/18qvdld

How To Install A Mod On Minecraft Windows

Step 1 – To install a modification, you'll need one first. Visit a Minecraft site or forum and download the particular Minecraft mod you'd like to use to your windows desktop. Pay attention before you download to check if the mod has its own installation requirements, (some mods require "Minecraft Forge" or "ModLoader" to work properly). Also check that the modification is the latest version, (earlier versions may have bugs or glitches that later mods have removed). When you've done all of this it's time for step 2.

Step 2 – To install your modification you're going to need an archive utility to open and edit the files and folders during installation. Most systems already have one installed, but if not, you can pick one up here at **WinRAR** (http://bit.ly/18qvjsS) or **7-Zip** (http://bit.ly/1bppywQ).

Step 3 – To install your mod, you'll need to locate minecraft.jar file (this is assuming that you've got the latest version of Minecraft installed on your machine). Click the Start button, and type " %appdata% " into the search window (without quotation marks but with one space before and another after the typed string) to get to Windows' application data folder. The folder '.minecraft' should be at the top. Open the folder titled 'bin', and look for the file "minecraft.jar" inside. If this file doesn't seem to be there, click the "Hidden folder" options of Windows file explorer, which should then reveal it.

Step 4 – Although it's not a required step, if you want you, can make a backup copy of the minecraft.jar file. This is done by simply right-clicking on this file and copy and then pasting it in the same folder with a different name. (This can be quickly changed back to its original name if everything goes wrong). Step 5 – Using your archive utility open the minecraft.jar file. Either by right-clicking and using "Open archive" in the windows drop down menu, or opening the file directly in your archive utility.

Step 6 – Now that you have the minecraft.jar folder open, simply drag the files from your "mod folder" to the now open minecraft.jar folder. This can be done either by using Alt+A or dragging all files individually.

Step 7 – Delete the file named META- INF, although this is a file that's included in the Mine-craft.jar folder, it's not one that's really needed and may cause problems with any new modification files that are added to the minecraft.jar folder.

Step 8 – Close all of the open files and launch the Minecraft game as normal. All going well the game should launch as normal and your new mods should work O.K. If not, try following all the above steps again, in case you'd left out a file from the modification folder. In the worst case scenario, it may be best to forget the modification and delete all the relevant files or simply reuse the original "minecraft.jar" folder that you backed- up.

MINECRAFT RESOURCES

Minecraft is one of the biggest games in the world today. A nearly infinite game world with a million possibilities of building and sometimes destruction. Yet, it is one of the most difficult games to just jump into and see what happens. The multiple updates, patches, and ever-changing world have made more than a few gamers shy away from this amazing title. Here we are going to outline some of the greatest resources available to new Minecraft players. So, without further ado and in no particular order, here are some of the most helpful sites for a Minecraft newbie.

Minecraft Wiki - The Minecraft wiki is billed as the "ultimate resource for all things Mine-craft". Of course, many people end up looking here as their first source for help in the world of Minecraft. They have well-written articles on just about subject in the Minecraft world.

Its sections are broken down into Gameplay, Popular and Useful Pages, Links, Servers, Version Development, as well as News and Events for the community. Aside from a nearly inexhaustible supply of articles about the game, the Minecraft Wiki has an extensive forum system where anyone can ask and answer questions. This is truly one of the greatest websites for new players because it is easy to navigate and has a familiar interface. Also, they have an area dedicated to tutorials and helping beginners. You should consider making this your very first stop on the way to Minecraft greatness. It can all be found here: http://bit.ly/196Xb5T

Minecraft Tutorial For Beginner's On Youtube - This tutorial, by COD4Nub, is one the greatest beginner videos on the internet for Minecraft players. It covers the very basic steps of the game such as joining a server and getting into the world. In my experience, these two steps are often ignored by other beginner tutorials, but COD4Nub really goes into depth. He films himself completing all of the introductory steps to the game, and provides some very helpful commentary along the way. The video then goes into your first day, teaching you how to navigate through your tools and how to find shelter. He also introduces you to the dreaded creeper, and gives you some rudimentary defense tactics. Overall this beginner's video series is probably the most helpful and in-depth look at Minecraft that you will find on the web.
http://bit.ly/IYyOxN

Minecraft Beginner's Handbook - Now, I know that most people will not be willing to buy a book for a video game in this era of online connectivity. However, you should consider purchasing this book for the sake of having an exclusive physical guide. The Minecraft Beginner's Handbook was developed by a company that spent months tracking down and inter-viewing the best Minecraft players from all over, for their greatest tips for beginning players. Also included are tips and comments from the creator of Minecraft, Notch, himself. This book is part of a series of books dedicated to helping gamers get the best experience from the game. While you have to pay for the book, you really do get your money's worth, and it will be a nice commemoration to the days when you were a Minecraft newbie. http://amzn.to/1d8mDr8

Minecraft Starter Guide and Extra Survival Tips [Walkthrough] - This article is the brain-child of one of the online gaming community's most well-respected and prolific authors, Mike Rose. This guide was published for fee on Diygamer.com back when Minecraft was starting to get some national attention in 2010. While it is not the most up- to-date resource that you will find on the web, there is still a plethora of useful starting information to be found in this starter guide. The guide covers all of the basics: shelter, forging, mining, and, of course, creepers. It is annotated with pictures that show everything that you need to know in order to get a good handle on the game. Also, when it comes to the Extra Survival Tips, Rose unleashes some serious gamer wisdom in the form proper torch placement and advanced mining techniques. All of things, and more, that will allow you to survive the torturous first days of being a miner. You can find this wonderful beginner's article at: http://bit.ly/1gMqxZ5

Absolute Beginner's Guide to Minecraft -Minecraft 101 -
This article is another fabulous way to begin your Minecraft
adventure. The author was not kidding when he writes
"absolute beginner's guide", because he literally shows you
how and where to properly download the game. He gives you
the pros and cons of playing online and offline, which is a
debate that still rages years after the game's release. This
guide does not rush you into taking cover immediately, and
instead encourages you to look around the world a little big
before you learn to live in fear of everything out there. There
are many links along the way that will take you deeper into
Minecraft 101, giving you a better understanding of the
essentials that you will need to get started and be successful in
the world. This guide can be found at: http://bit.ly/1gevsob

PlanetMinecraft - While on the surface this may look similar
to the other beginner Mine-craft guides, this one has a special
place on this list of beginner's guides because it goes through
the tedious process of revealing and discussing the Minecraft
servers. This is a huge advantage to people who, like most
newbies, have no idea what they are doing in terms of
choosing a server. Do you want to know the differences
between the big three types of Player versus Player, Faction
Player versus Player, and Economy servers? Then you should
check this site out while you are downloading the game. It is
packed with easy to read information and tips, and will help
you get off to a great start in the Minecraft world. This
information can be found here: http://bit.ly/1bnqbWA

Now that we have covered some of the most comprehensive
guides to beginner action on Minecraft, we need to take a look
at some of the sites dedicated to the more advanced players in
the world. These guides will teach you how to maximize
every minute of game-play while achieving new limits in
every mode.

Advanced Goals - IGNIGN has been a great source of game guides for over a decade. There is little wonder in the fact that they were one of the first groups to unleash a comprehensive end game guide. In particular, this guide provides beginning end game advice. In other words, this is a necessary first step to becoming an advanced player. This guide starts by telling you which mods you should download in order to gain meaningful extensions of the base Minecraft game. It then covers aspects of the world such as setting up a permanent residence and experimenting with redstone and other in-game mechanisms. Overall, this guide is a good first step in the long end game process that awaits advances players. All of this can be found online at: http://bit.ly/IYzrHz

Minecraft: Advanced: Wonder How To - This is not an article nor is it a wiki per se, it is a collection of various topics and links to helpful videos that have been gathered from all over the web. If you have a specific goal or question in mind that requires a finer knowledge of the game, make this one of your stops along the path. The best part about this site is that it is an amalgamation of gamer knowledge; a resource by the gamer and for the gamer. Also to be found on this site is a comprehensive list of interesting minecraft skins (think Skyrim) as well as some goofy additions to the game. All in all, this is a good site that every advanced player should visit at least once. This site can be found at: http://bit.ly/1bnqmS2

Minecraft: The Ultimate Redstone Guide Series- by Magix -
One of the most prolific and underrated Minecraft Youtube
contributors goes by the name Magix. While he is not as
famous as other Minecraft such as BrenyBeast, his guide really
takes the viewer step by step through his material. His
Ultimate Redstone Guide is a three part series that explores
one of most valuable commodities available for trade:
Redstone. By having a perfect understanding of redstone, you
increase your chances of being economically viable in
Minecraft. This, in turn, allows you to purchase and trade at
high levels and acquire goods that would take much longer to
receive under normal circumstances. Even if you choose to go
with one of the more mainstream Youtubers, it is absolutely
pertinent that you receive a background in redstone
production and trade. This video servers can be found here:
http://bit.ly/1eX3ycG

MinecraftDL - This entry almost needs no introduction
because it is so well known in the Minecraft community.
Minecraft DL features the largest dedicated minecraft
download community available on the internet. Here you will
find all of the latest and most famous downloadable content to
make your Minecraft experience even more enjoyable. As of
the last check-in, there were fifteen pages of downloadable
content available for all gamers. While it is important to
remember to check the tags on each and every download so
you do not get a bad download or a potential virus (they are
very rare), you will come away with some of the most
interesting mods that have ever been created for a videogame.
This web-site can be found at: http://bit.ly/1d201Id

The Gigantic Guide For Building Minecraft - If you are wondering where the biggest online community of Minecraft contributors, players, and advanced informational guides can be found, then you need to look no further than Reddit. At first, this may seem rather counter intuitive, after all Reddit is a bit scrambled and disconnected when it comes to some of their forums. However, when the title says "Gigantic Guide" they mean it. On this Reddit page, you will find links to over fifty of the most famous and successful web pages of all Minecraft players. They are even broken down into general building topics, circles and spheres, furniture and interior designing, block combinations and patterns, underwater building, arches and columns, and then miscellaneous information.

Under each of these headings, you will find the best information from all of the greatest Minecraft contributors. SkyDoesMinecraft, Captain Sparkelz, Antvenom, and JeromeASF are all well-known Minecraft players that have written advanced material that is only found on this site. These are the same people that made scale models of Hogwarts and the Game of Thrones World. These are the tips and tricks that will send you to the very next level.

Once you have read through the basic advanced material that was outlined in the previous headings, you should come here immediately to get started on the massive projects that gain renown in the Minecraft community. If you want to see what you will be capable of building once you have reviewed the Reddit material, you should go to R/Minecraft and see some truly wondrous architecture. In the meantime, all of the high level. Advanced material can be found here: http://bit.ly/1bmZCO6

Hopefully, this list of reputable websites has given you some options to consider if you are looking to enjoy the vast game world that is Minecraft. These are all wonderful resources for both new and seasoned players. Keep in mind that while this list is extensive, it is certainly not exhaustive. There are always new sources coming in from all over the web to con-sider when looking for the easiest ways to begin your adventure as well as when you seek to take your abilities to the next level. It is highly encouraged for you to take part in the online forums and discussions about Minecraft.

By doing so, you may come across more valuable tips and tricks that are not yet public knowledge or have not been well-documented enough to garner attention. After all, it is not only a game, it is an entire interactive world that is best cultivated when you realize that it is a dynamic place that is very much like the real world. Remember to have fun and watch out for the wrathful creepers!

Thanks

For Purchasing "Minecraft – The Ultimate Players Guide To Minecraft"

We at Ultimate App Guidebooks really hope you enjoyed this book and we'd love to read your comments. When you get to the last page of this book on your device you'll be asked to leave a review. Please do so as it helps to get this book in front of more readers.

If you're a big fan of Candy Crush Saga, why not grab a copy of our other guide book "Candy Crush Saga – The Ultimate Players Guide To Beating Candy Crush"

http://amzn.to/1jx5hZA

CPSIA information can be obtained at www.ICGtesting.com
Printed in the USA
LVOW12s1523180614

390647LV00022B/1433/P

[8]